We used to talk,
We used to play together,
We shared our lives,
No more...

Invisible

by

Diana R Fiore

Second Edition
ISBN: 979-8-9867993-0-8

Cover Design and Illustrations by Diana R. Fiore

Published under Diana R. Fiore

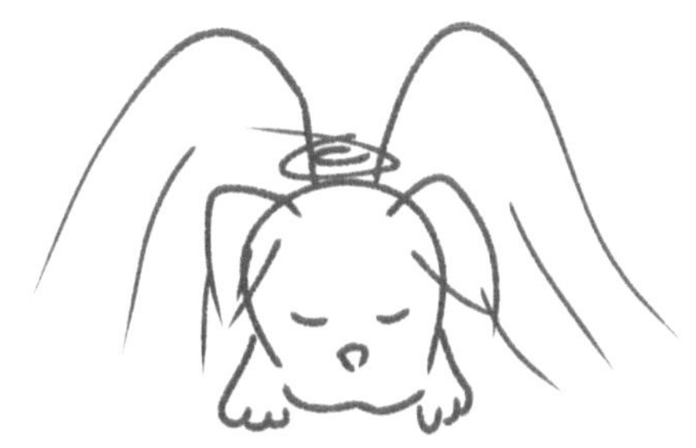

To Nini,

My best friend
of 10 short years,
and counting.
May we meet again ♡

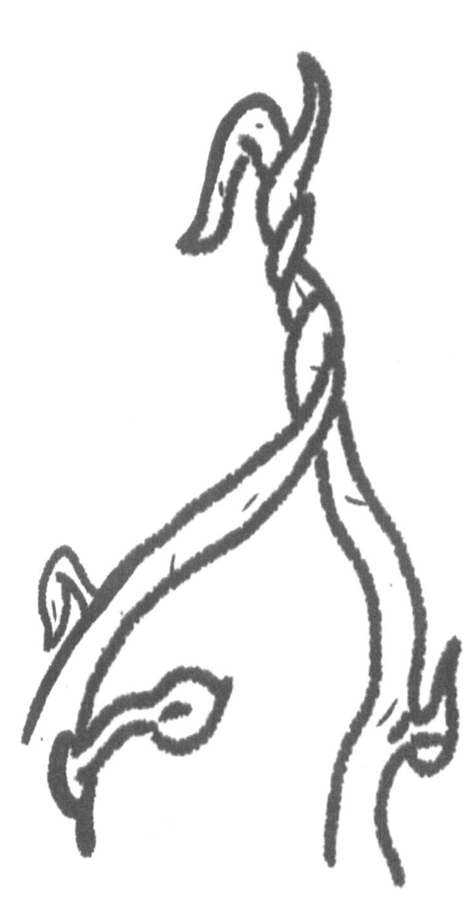

Mother and I were
inseparable
She taught me
new things
every day

She taught me about food...

She showed me the world...

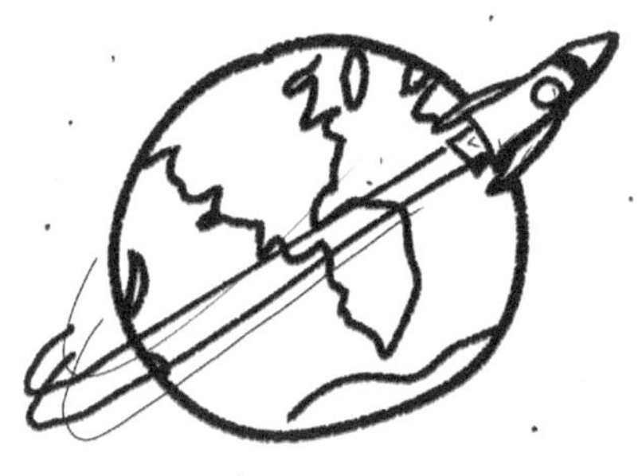

We loved playing

and going out together.

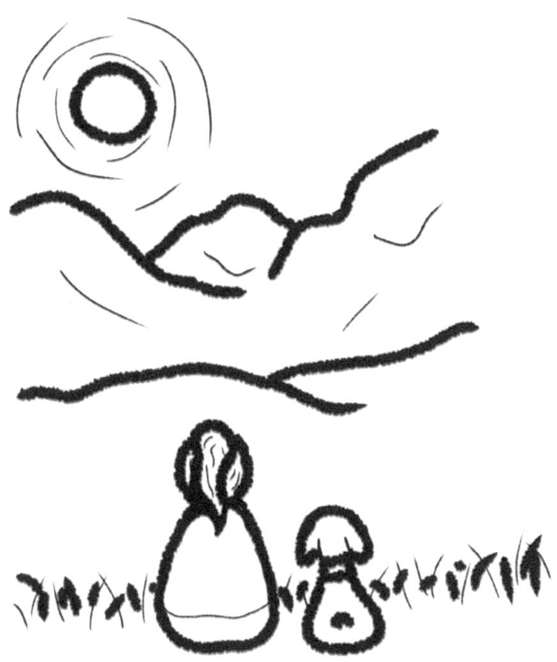

She would hold me
close to her
when I
needed comfort

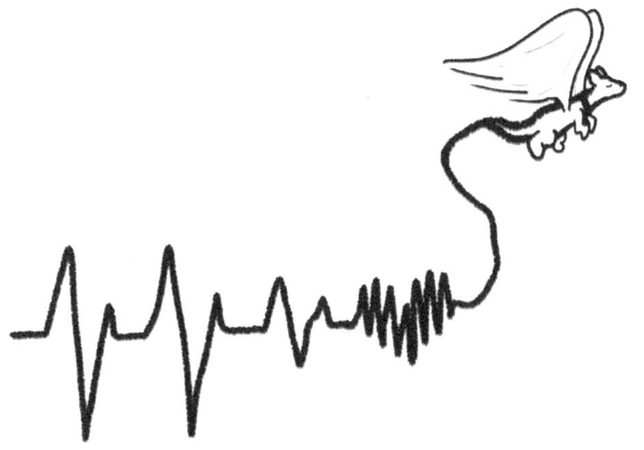

But one day,
it all stopped...

Mother was holding me.
She sang to me,
and all I wanted to do
was

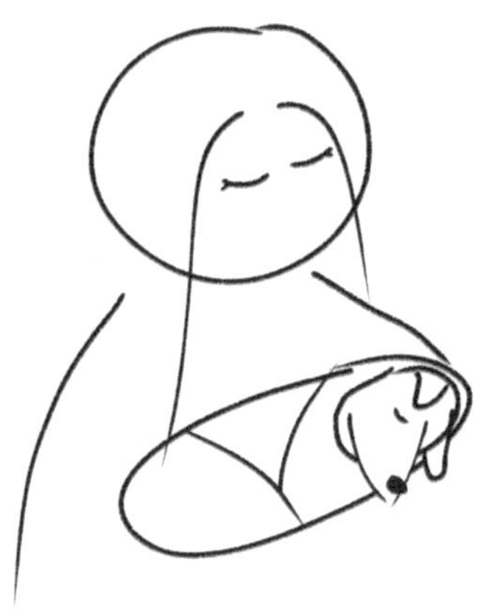

to look at her...

To let her know I
was listening

but
I
couldn't
turn
my
head

She gently swayed me
back and forth,
like she used to
when she sang to me

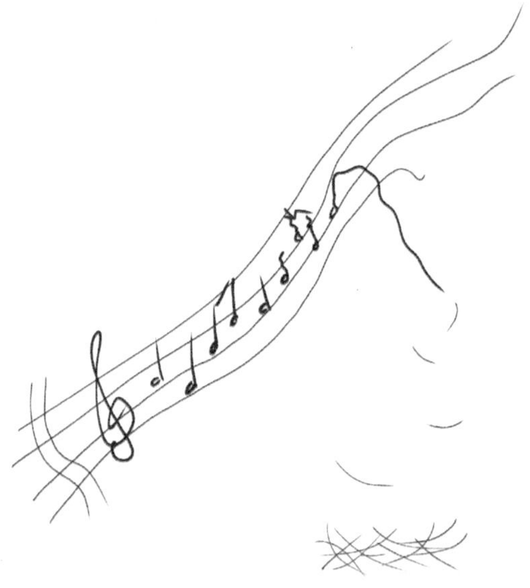

her voice began to crack

On that day,
she set me down
and looked at me
for the last time.

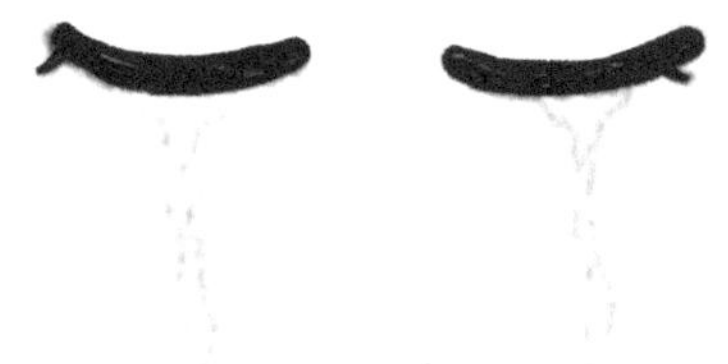

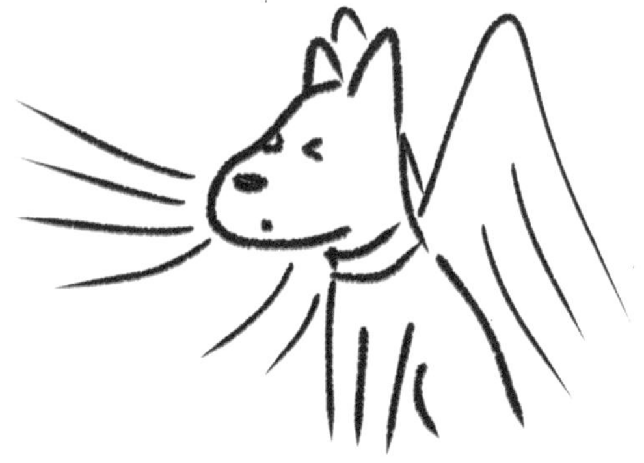

I tried to get her
attention in many ways,
but all my attempts
were in vain.

She became good at ignoring me.

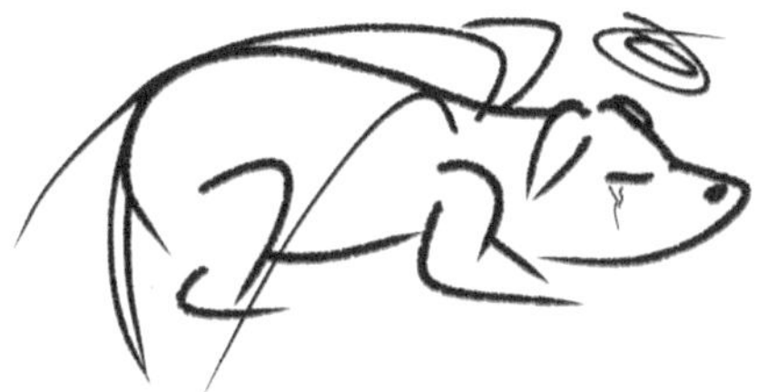

She cried at night.
My attempts
to comfort her
didn't work
anymore

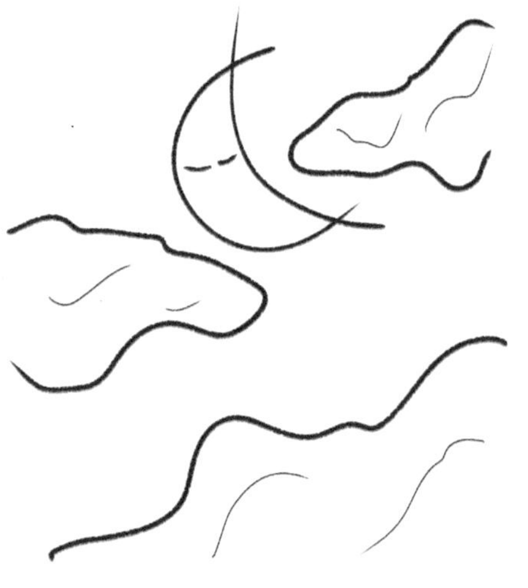

I

was

invisible

For many days,
I kept her company.
I wanted to be
acknowledged.

But more than
anything,
I wanted her
to feel better.

As years passed,

I grew

accustomed to being

ignored

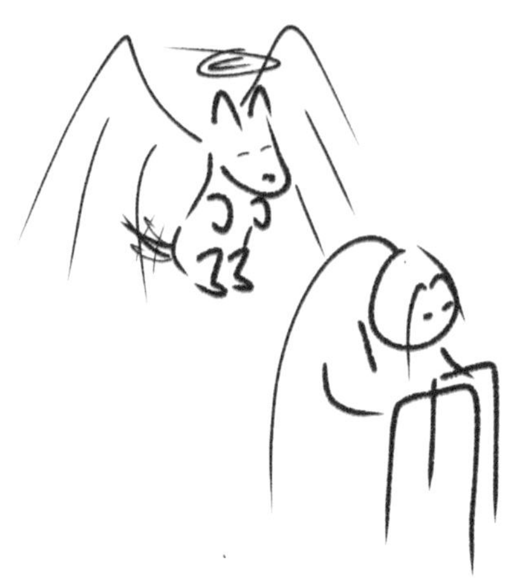

But I never stopped caring for her

We grew older together.

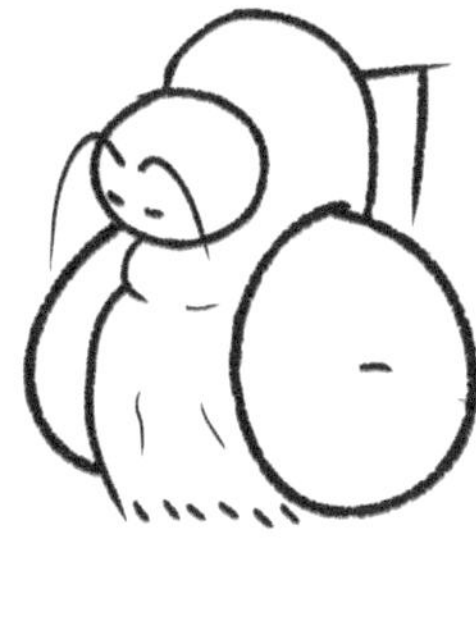

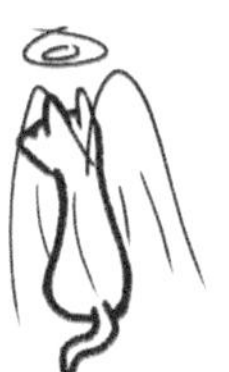

With age,

She became

sedentary

We moved houses,
the spaces kept
getting smaller

Made it easier to
watch over her

Years passed.
Mother's health
rapidly deteriorated.

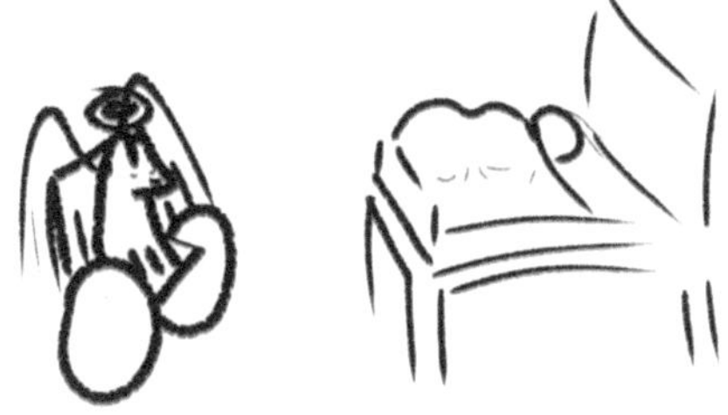

We took turns,
Bed
and
Wheelchair

Mother didn't cry
much
anymore

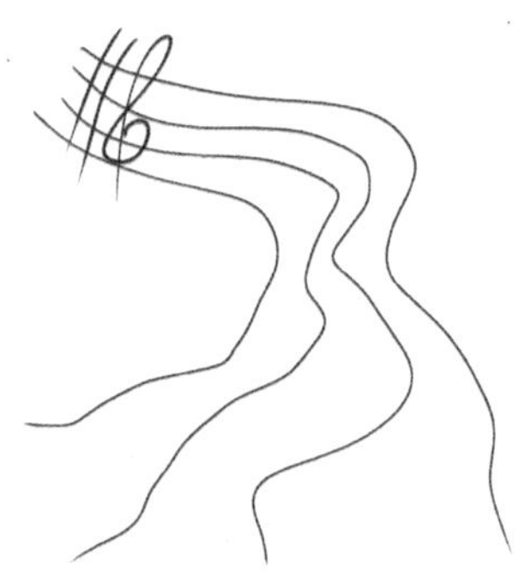

Crying is not the only
thing she stopped
doing.

I began to wonder
if she had lost her
voice

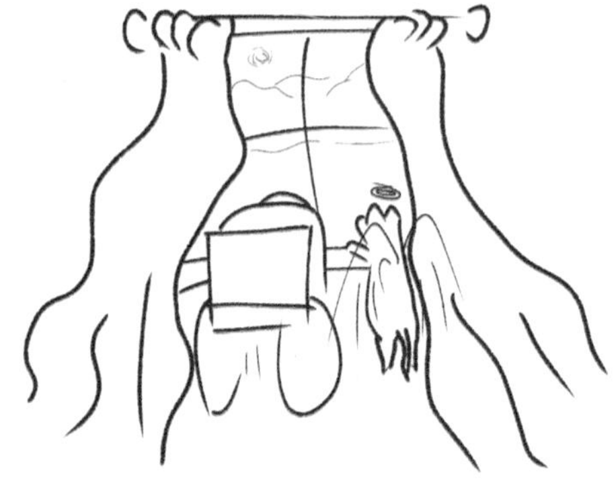

Beside her by the
window,
I would imagine her
pointing out new things
through the glass

One morning,
I saw her standing

It had been many
years since I last
saw her walk.

She was
slowly heading
toward me

I looked up at her,

the unimaginable
finally happened,

she looked at me

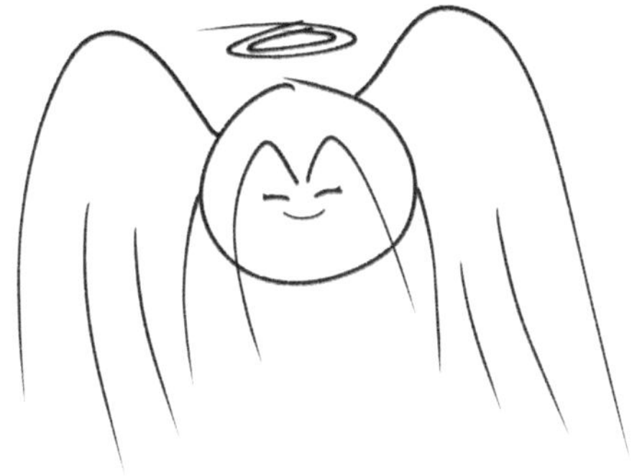

She

smiled

at

me

She carried me

once more,

pressed me against her

And with my head
on her shoulder,
she sang to me
As we flew away
together

We will talk,
We will play together,
We will share our lives,
Once again

♡

please, take care

www.ingramcontent.com/pod-product-compliance
Lightning Source LLC
LaVergne TN
LVHW090540110826
845146LV00003B/1201
9798986799308